Common Core State Standards

Building a Solid Foundation

Janet McCoid

Copyright ©2011 by Janet M. McCoid
ALL RIGHTS RESERVED.

No part of this publication may be reproduced, stored in a retrieval system, or transmitted in any form or by any means, electronic, mechanical, photocopying, recording, or otherwise, without prior written permission. Reproduction prohibitions do not apply to the forms contained in this product when reproduced for personal use.

ISBN-13: 978-1460907016

ISBN-10: 1460907019

Table of Contents

Chapter 1   Common Core State Standards
A Brief Introduction. 1

Chapter 2   Preparing for Change 3

Chapter 3   Conducting a Focused Professional Development
Needs Assessment...25

Chapter 4   Conducting a Gap Analysis......................................35

Chapter 5   Identifying Gaps Within the Curriculum…….…….45

Chapter 6   Analyzing Current Student Work Samples
to Find Evidence of Common Core State
Standards Rigor……………………………………..53

> "Education is not the filling of a pail, but the lighting of a fire."
>
> *William Butler Yeats*

About the Author

Janet McCoid is a National Board Certified Teacher who currently resides in New Jersey with her husband, three children, and two eccentric Shih Tzu's. She has extensive experience as a classroom teacher, instructional coach, and author. As an educational consultant, Mrs. McCoid has conducted workshops at many local, state and national conferences. She also enjoys developing educational products and has received numerous awards for her contributions to the field of education. She has a bachelor's degree in elementary education from Pace University, a master's degree in teaching with a specialization in early childhood advanced curriculum and teaching from Kean University, and a master's degree in teaching from Walden University with a specialization in elementary mathematics.

Terrence, thank you for always supporting my hopes and dreams.

Chapter 1

Common Core State Standards

A Brief Introduction

In 2009, The National Governors Association and the Council of Chief State School Officers coordinated a state-led effort to construct a coherent and focused tool designed to transform instruction and learning. The goal was to create a clear, consistent framework that would ensure students were developing the knowledge and skills necessary for success in college and the workforce. Many stakeholders were involved in the creation of this document, now known as Common Core State Standards. This framework incorporates lessons learned from past experiences in education, information gathered from available research, and input from many highly qualified individuals.

Research has suggested many individual state academic standards are typically "a mile wide and an inch deep". In other words, an overabundance of topics seem to be taught at every grade level, leaving little time for students and teachers to focus on particularly significant areas.

The intent of Common Core State Standards is to provide consistent, high expectations for each grade level. This is accomplished by describing the "what" in terms of critical content taught at each grade level, not the "how". The objective of instruction is to ensure that core understandings are solid and well developed. Students dig deeply into problem solving methods and strategies as opposed to focusing on "answer-getting" methods. Grade level expectations are now higher, fewer, and clearer with evidence of coherent progression from one grade level to the next, as well as within each grade level band. These expectations foster rigorous teaching and deep learning. The intent is to move the focus away from simply covering material, which implies teaching an objective and moving on, regardless of whether or not there is any evidence of student understanding. Common Core State Standards support intentional, rigorous teaching, and optimal student understanding. They provide teachers and students with opportunities to organize and explain thinking, investigate ideas, analyze errors, and apply knowledge while engaging in multiple approaches to problem solving.

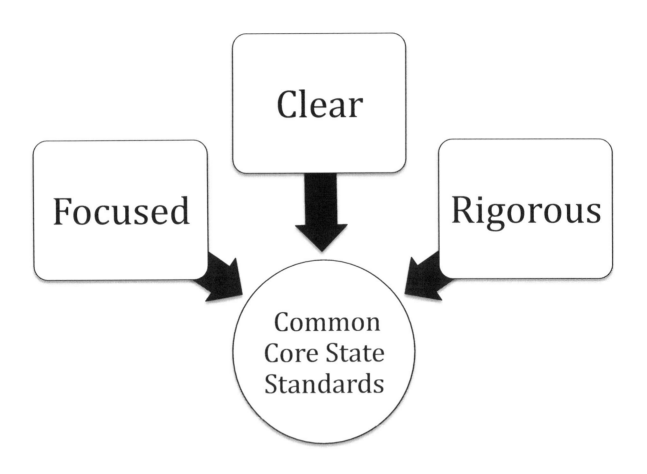

Chapter 2

Preparing for Change

Change. This one simple word has been known to evoke a wide range of emotions. In some, the thought of change brings about anxiety and stress. In others, change may awaken feelings of excitement and anticipation.

It is helpful to acknowledge the fact that change can be uncomfortable. It is also helpful to explore and prepare for specific components of any change that will be taking place. Strategies that can be implemented to assist with adapting to new expectations, responsibilities and ideas are best thought of in advance. Whenever initiating change, it is helpful to provide time prior to the actual transition period so that people have an opportunity to think about, consider, and become comfortable with the change before it actually happens. The activities in this chapter have been designed to help facilitate the change process.

Creating an Introductory Workshop Focused on Exploring the Common Core State Standards

As participants enter the training session, provide an icebreaker activity such as the Common Core State Standard Word Find (Activity 1) or the word scramble maze entitled Follow the Path to the Common Core State Standards (Activity 2). Providing participants with a task that is familiar and comfortable can help ease the anxiety that change sometimes fosters.

- Icebreaker 1 (Word Find)
  This icebreaker contains terms relevant to the Common Core State Standards, and can stimulate thinking about various components of the Common Core.

- Icebreaker 2 (Word Scramble - Follow the Path to the Common Core)
  This icebreaker can be used as a way to encourage the reluctant teacher to "move" toward the Common Core State Standards in a symbolic fashion.

Icebreaker #1
The Common Core State Standards
Word Find

```
X Y W F R C S S H A U J V X G D U O D Z
A U S A R S U Y I V R O R N I O Q O H U
S H E O Y A M N I N O E I O K M G K F T
Z L T O O E M V V Q T H R I N A Q L V F
C O N S I S T E N T C B L T O I J O M Z
K Q X T K C K X W A Z D A A W N C T D P
E K X F M E X R E O H M X C L S C P T S
S G Z P K L I T J K R O I I E J S Z K R
S E C N E D I V E E T K C L D N R R E G
G N I D N A T S R E D N U P G C A A D N
A R O O S U I D O V Z V R P E M L E J I
N L E I E U Y A G E N I R A H I E Z W N
A N I W T Z O O I E W U B C S P G D N R
H O I G E A A R R Z C E N T E J F P H A
P K X W N F T L O K P E I R S L A O G E
D V W R V E D C Y G B C T Z Y D I U B L
N L B O Y J D T E L I X V L E H H U S N
J I R A A J W T G P O R C L U S T E R S
V G Q Z A P X I V Z X R N B F P K S P R
U X E V U Y D S E C H E V F W D V V J X
```

WORD BANK

ALIGNED	FRAMEWORK
APPLICATION	GOALS
BENCHMARKS	KNOWLEDGE
CLEAR	LEARNING
CLUSTERS	REALISTIC
CONSISTENT	RIGOR
DEEPER	RIGOROUS
DOMAINS	TEACHING
EVIDENCE	UNDERSTANDING
EXPECTATIONS	
FEWER	

Icebreaker #2
Follow the Path to Common Core State Standards!
Unscramble each word!

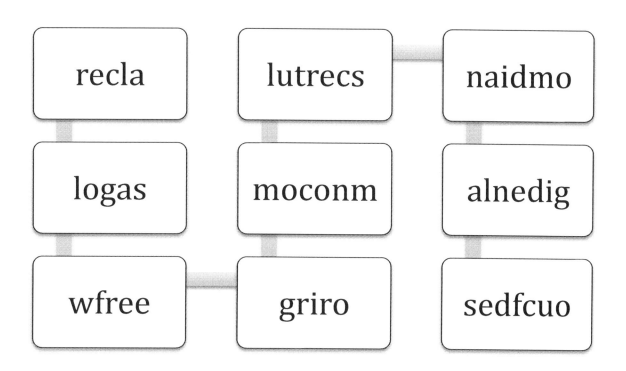

recla	lutrecs	naidmo
logas	moconm	alnedig
wfree	griro	sedfcuo

You made it!

Answer Key
Icebreaker #1
The Common Core State Standards
Word Find

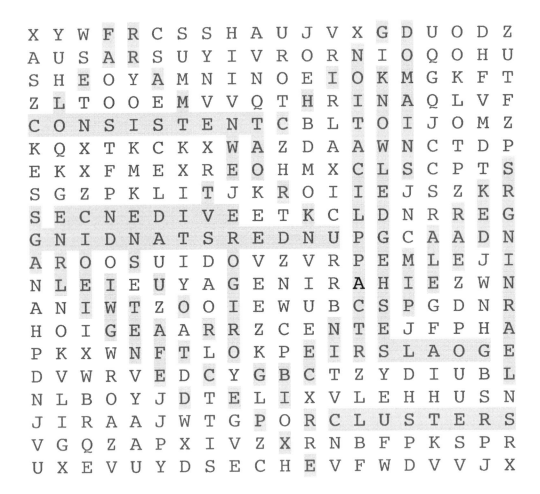

Answer Key
Icebreaker #2

clear	cluster	domain
goals	common	aligned
fewer	rigor	focused

Exploration Activities

The following activities have been designed to provide opportunities to explore change and the Common Core State Standards. They can be used independently, or can be combined to create a more in-depth workshop.

❖ Activity 1 (Common Core Land Game)

This activity consists of a simple and effective board game that reviews components of the Common Core State Standards and provides a healthy dose of humor. Simply photocopy the game board and a set of cards for each group of 2 - 4 people, and include a copy of the instruction sheet for game play. This game can be used to either introduce the Common Core State Standards or refresh the memories of those who have some experience working with them.

❖ Activity 2 (Discussion Starters)

This activity consists of using discussion starter cards to encourage conversation about Common Core State Standards. Photocopy the questions so that you have one set for each group. Each group should contain less than 5 participants in order to encourage sustained, active participation. Provide several minutes for groups to engage in a discussion about the topics followed by several minutes for sharing with the larger group at the conclusion of the activity.

❖ Activity 3 (Concern Circle)

This activity provides participants with the opportunity to discuss and record concerns about all things related to Common Core State Standards. The information gathered can be used to drive future professional development sessions.

❖ Activity 4 (Areas of Concern)

This activity includes a workspace for small groups to identify any areas of concern they may have in terms of implementation of the Common Core State Standards. Once concerns are identified and recorded, they can be adequately addressed.

❖ Activity 5 (Reflecting on Change)

This questionnaire provides either individuals or groups with an opportunity to explore thoughts and feelings on change. This type of reflection can assist participants in recognizing how they respond to change, how they feel about change, and strategies they can utilize to plan and prepare for change.

Stages of Change

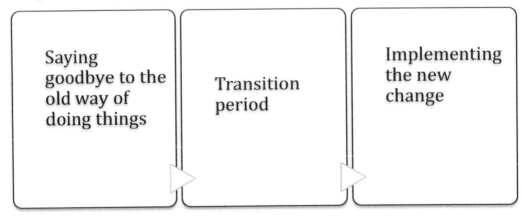

Activity 1
Common Core Land Board Game

Games can provide an opportunity for an increase in participation, interest, and motivation. Common Core Land is a game that provides a chance to debate, expand upon and review key components of Common Core State Standards in a friendly, fun format. Misconceptions, misunderstandings and confusion can be gently addressed through game play. Just as a teacher differentiates instruction for students, the blank card template provides an opportunity for the facilitator to differentiate game play for participants, as well. The game can be customized according to topic, grade level, or subject area.

Team building is another positive outcome of this type of experience, too. Through playing a game, participants have the opportunity to develop the tools they need to work collaboratively in a group setting. Listening skills can be fine-tuned, and working with a shared goal can encourage discussions between group members.

To prepare for game play:

- Copy one game board for every 2 - 4 players
- Copy one set of cards per game board
  (Use colored copy paper if possible)
- Cut out the game cards and place them in a zip top bag.
  (This will help to keep the decks separated)
- Provide one game piece for each player to move around the board. A variety of buttons, small multi-colored chips or different coins can be used. Store the game pieces in the bag with the deck of cards.

Common Core Land Board Game

Object of the Game:
Be the first player to land on the Finish space at the end of the path.

Number of Players: 2 – 4 players

Items Needed for Game Play:
  ❖ One Common Core Land game board
  ❖ One game piece per player
  ❖ One deck of Common Core Land cards

Rules:
1. Place your game piece on Start.
2. Pick a player to go first.
3. The first player chooses a card and follows the instructions.
4. Players may occupy the same space.
5. The first player to land on Finish wins

Welcome to Common Core Land!

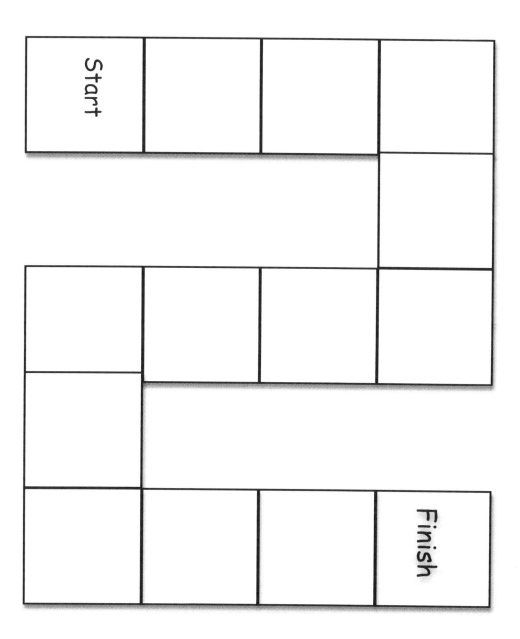

You are using lesson plans from 1986. Move backward 3 spaces.	You have never heard of Common Core State Standards. Move backward two spaces.
You know a standard is what students should know and be able to do. Move forward 2 spaces.	As you are writing math plans, you recall that clusters are groups of related standards. Move forward 1 space.

A colleague is asking questions during a Common Core training session. You roll your eyes and sigh…LOUDLY. Move backward 3 spaces.	You consider all 8 mathematical practices as you plan your lessons. Move forward 3 spaces, or change places with another player.
Parents are requesting information about the Common Core State Standards. Your school provides a parent workshop to explain the details. Move forward 2 spaces.	You write in your notes that a domain consists of larger groups of related standards. Move forward 1 space.

You decide to compare the "old" standards with the Common Core State Standards. Move forward 2 spaces.	You tell a colleague that the Common Core State Standards are just more concepts that need to be covered. Move backward 2 spaces.
A teacher tells you they will continue to use the same dittos they have been using for the last 10 years. You ask for copies. Move backward 3 spaces.	You begin to investigate where the gaps are in the current curriculum when looking through the lens of the Common Core State Standards. Move forward 2 spaces.

You decide to hoard all of the old workbooks you can so you will be prepared when your district implements the Common Core State Standards. Move backward 3 spaces.	You are ready to teach fewer, clearer and higher standards! Move forward 4 spaces!
Several colleagues don't understand some of the math Common Core State Standards. You take the time to work through the areas of difficulty with them. Move forward 2 spaces.	You cannot find your copy of the Common Core State Standards. Again. Move backward 1 space.

You have a chance to attend a workshop on increasing academic rigor. You register and attend. Move forward 2 spaces.	You present a workshop that focuses on exploring content deeply with students. Move forward 2 spaces.
You are caught texting during a Professional Development meeting. Move backward 5 spaces!	You are thinking about the types of assessments you can use to monitor student thinking, understanding, and application. Move forward 3 spaces.

You begin talking with your grade level team about how to address some of the new ideas found in the Common Core State Standards. Move forward 2 spaces.	A colleague asks if you would like to review the Common Core State Standards together. You agree and set up a date and time to meet. Move forward 1 space.
A student teacher asks to borrow a copy of the Common Core Standards. You reply, "My dog ate them." Move backward 2 spaces.	You know MD stands for Measurement and Data. Move forward 1 space.

You are asked to review the current curriculum through the lens of the Common Core State Standards. You diligently work through the process. Move forward 4 spaces.	You spend a relaxing afternoon with your family. Move forward 3 spaces.
You know NBT stands for Number and Operations in Base Ten. Move forward 1 space.	Your supervisor reminds you that there is a Common Core State Standards meeting after school. You fake an illness and leave school early. Move backward 3 spaces.

Blank Card Template

Activity 2
Discussion Starters

Share your thoughts about each item below.

1. Describe what the Common Core State Standards will look like.

2. Describe what the Common Core State Standards will sound like.

3. Describe what the Common Core State Standards will feel like.

4. Describe what the Common Core State Standards will accomplish.

Activity 3
Concern Circle

Draw a large circle and write the word "Concerns" in the center. Ask participants to write any concerns they may have about the transition to the Common Core State Standards on a sticky note. These notes can then be placed within the circle. This provides an outlet for concerns, a voice for all participants, and a recording of issues you may need to address in future workshops.

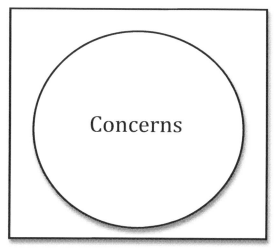

At a future workshop, participants can sort the concerns posted within the circle into categories. This will help organize the areas of need, and will provide data that can be accessed when planning future training sessions. The concerns can be sorted into different categories. For example, understanding, training, content, implementation, and materials are all appropriate categories to consider. The Areas of Concern worksheet (Activity 4) is another recording sheet that can be utilized in either small group settings or by individuals. The Reflections on Change template (Activity 5) can help individuals take a personal inventory of their feelings and thoughts about particular changes.

Activity 4
Areas of Concern

| Materials | Understanding Content |

| Implementation | Training |

| Other |

Activity 5
Reflections on Change

1. Identify the change.

2. What is the essence of the change?

3. Consider how this change will affect you

    - Emotionally

    - Spiritually

    - Individually

    - As an organization

4. What steps can be taken now to prepare for the change?

5. What positive differences do you expect to see once the change occurs?

6. What challenges do you expect from this change?

7. What resources will you need to help transition through this change?

8. What training will you need to prepare for this change?

Chapter 3

Conducting a Focused Professional Development Needs Assessment

Before you can determine the direction you want to head in, you first need to know where you are, and where you want to be. By conducting a needs assessment, precise, meaningful professional development plans can be created by and for staff. It is critical to take the time to conduct an in-depth analysis to determine professional training needs so that precious time and resources aren't squandered. By including staff in the professional development planning process, personal and collective responsibility for learning is encouraged.

This chapter contains resources that will assist with this important process.

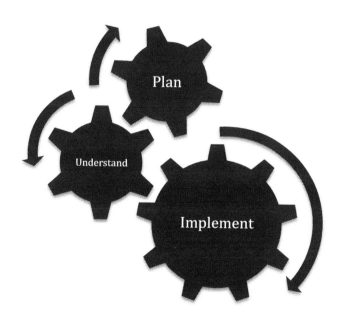

Where Do I Begin?

It is important to provide staff with opportunities to describe their needs and concerns prior to planning and scheduling professional development sessions. This process can pinpoint particular areas of concern. In an effort to maximize the effectiveness of professional development sessions, an effective agenda is critical. The time available to explore and understand the spirit of the Common Core State Standards is precious!

The basic purpose of an agenda is to openly communicate important information. The objective of any workshop session should be clearly stated and adhered to, ensuring important components of the training are included. The agenda can also serve as a checklist, keeping both the presenter and the participants on track.

If possible, distribute the agenda prior to the workshop, so that participants have an opportunity to formulate questions and gather resources pertinent to the topic being discussed. When participants receive an agenda prior to a workshop, the seriousness of the meeting is conveyed. An agenda reinforces the idea that participants are expected to be prepared with pertinent questions and insights related to the workshop.

Agendas can be written in bullet or list form. Each item included should directly relate to the objective of the meeting, and should be brief. Make a serious attempt to follow the agenda. It is easy to become sidetracked and waste precious time on items that are not relevant.

Post a meeting reminder by the staff sign in area.

It is helpful to include a section entitled "notes" on the bottom of the agenda, as it makes it clear that participants are expected to record important information. Agendas can be sent to staff via email or can be placed in individual mailboxes prior to the meeting. It is helpful to send a reminder email a day before the workshop is to occur. This conveys the importance of the meeting, and serves as a gentle reminder to come prepared.

When preparing to facilitate a workshop, writing and referring to a list can help keep you organized. Check off each item as you complete the task, and keep the list with all of your workshop materials. When your materials are centrally located, the chances of losing a paper or forgetting to complete an important task decreases.

To Do List

- **Reserve a meeting place**
- **Reserve technology needed for the presentation**
- **Create a clear, concise agenda**
- **Gather necessary materials (Chart paper, sticky notes, highlighters, pencils, paper, handouts)**
- **Send a reminder email/memo to attendees**
- **Distribute a copy of the agenda prior to the workshop.**

Sample Agenda

Date: April 17th
Time: 3:30 - 4:30pm
Location: Library

Please bring:
Sticky notes, highlighters, a copy of the curriculum map

Meeting Objectives

- Review of specific goals
- Expected outcomes
- Roles and responsibilities
- Timelines
- Questions
- Summary

Notes:

Agenda

Date:
Time:
Location:

Please bring:

Meeting Objectives:

Notes:

Gathering Data

There are several quick and efficient ways to determine the professional development needs of staff members. Surveys, questionnaires, and worksheets can be utilized to collect thoughtful responses from staff. It is helpful to provide time during a staff meeting for teachers to complete any form being used for this purpose. Several different surveys, worksheets and questionnaires have been included within this chapter.

Participants may provide more feedback if they are not required to write their name on the survey. A sign in sheet can be used as evidence that participants had the opportunity to complete the questionnaire or survey being utilized.

Surveys can be collected in a large envelope or folder that is passed around the room. Simply attach an attendance list to the front of the envelope or folder, and ask participants to sign next to their name indicating they have completed the survey.

Be sure to analyze the survey results within a reasonable time period and report the results to the stakeholders. If staff sees that opinions, thoughts, suggestions and ideas are valued, active participation in and implementation of professional development training will most likely increase.

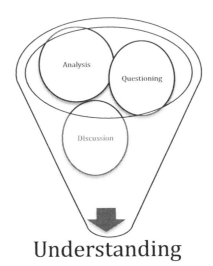

Understanding

Common Core State Standards Inventory

What I know	**What I want to know**
What I found out	**Further questions**

Common Core State Standards

Professional Development Needs Assessment Questionnaire #1

Please take a moment to answer the questions below. Your answers will assist us as we design training opportunities for staff. We value your input!

1. What specific questions do you have about the Common Core State Standards?

2. Indicate which professional development sessions would be most helpful, in order of preference, with 1 being your first choice.

   _____ Conducting a gap analysis between what is required by state standards versus Common Core State Standards

   _____ Conducting a gap analysis between the current curriculum and the Common Core State Standards

   _____ Identifying classroom resources that address the Common Core State Standards

   _____ Identifying areas of focus new to a grade level

   _____ Determining which standards have been omitted or modified

   _____ Creating a curriculum map based on the Common Core State Standards

   _____ Unpacking and implementing specific components of Common Core State Standards

   _____ Creating concrete examples of focus areas and concepts outlined within the Common Core State Standards

   _____ Creating/identifying formal and informal assessments that align with the Common Core State Standards

3. What are your concerns about implementing the Common Core State Standards?

Common Core State Standards
Professional Development Needs Assessment Questionnaire #2

Please indicate your level of interest in each of the following presenters listed.

Presenters	Strong Interest	Interest	Little/No Interest
Instructional Coaches	☐	☐	☐
Colleagues	☐	☐	☐
District Supervisors/Directors	☐	☐	☐
Consultants	☐	☐	☐
Principals	☐	☐	☐
Community Members	☐	☐	☐
University Faculty/State Representatives	☐	☐	☐
Other			

Please rate your interest in each of the presentation formats listed below.

PRESENTATION FORMATS	Strong Interest	Some Interest	Little/No Interest
Workshops including active, whole group participation	☐	☐	☐
Small group work sessions	☐	☐	☐
Lectures	☐	☐	☐
Demonstrations	☐	☐	☐
Real-world application examples presented by peer groups	☐	☐	☐
Keynote presentations followed by break-out sessions	☐	☐	☐
Video Clips/group discussions	☐	☐	☐
Webinar/web-based learning	☐	☐	☐
PD that includes mixed grade levels	☐	☐	☐
PD that includes same grade levels	☐	☐	☐

Common Core State Standards

Professional Development Needs Assessment Questionnaire #3

Professional Development Opportunities	Strong Interest	Some Interest	Little/No Interest
Conducting a gap analysis between what is required by state standards versus Common Core State Standards	☐	☐	☐
Conducting a gap analysis between the current curriculum and the Common Core State Standards	☐	☐	☐
Identifying classroom resources that address the Common Core State Standards	☐	☐	☐
Identifying areas of focus new to a grade level	☐	☐	☐
Determining which standards have been omitted or modified	☐	☐	☐
Creating a curriculum map based on the Common Core State Standards	☐	☐	☐
Unpacking and implementing specific components of the Common Core State Standards	☐	☐	☐
Creating concrete examples of focus areas and concepts outlined within the Common Core State Standards	☐	☐	☐
Creating/identifying formal and informal assessments that align with the Common Core State Standards	☐	☐	☐

Suggestions:

Comments:

Chapter 4

Conducting a Gap Analysis

Comparing State Standards to Common Core State Standards
This chapter includes a collection of strategies and templates created to assist with comparing and contrasting the academic requirements found in current state standards and Common Core State Standards.

Overview

It is important to have a simple system in place when conducting a gap analysis. The more complicated the system is, the more likely it is to fail.

To begin, create small manageable teams that can work together to complete specific components of the gap analysis. Teams can be organized in many ways. For example, you can create teams by grade level (grade 2 teachers, or teachers from a variety of grades combined) by standard, or by content area.

When possible, assign a point person or facilitator for each group. This individual can be responsible for organizing the work as it is being completed, and can relay questions and concerns to administration. A leadership role can assist with maintaining the structure of a group and also confirm the importance of the work. Additional jobs such as Researcher or Recorder may be assigned to group members. When people are given a specific responsibility, the likelihood that they will participate increases.

Avoid the intricate use of technology, and keep the task at hand clear, focused, and simple. Groups should be small so that active participation is fostered. Keep directions concise and provide an example or model whenever possible. The facilitator may circulate throughout the groups as they work, offering encouragement, support and guidance. It isn't enough to simply read over the Common Core State Standards once, twice, or three times. Teachers need to consider the spirit of each standard and determine how it fits into overall big ideas. Through the process of discovering and discussing what the intended outcomes of implementing the Common Core State Standards will be, understanding will increase. Don't assume that every teacher knows and is comfortable with the depth of each standard. Make time for discussion, exploration, research, and experimentation. This critical process takes time, energy, and patience.

A few words on setting professional development goals:
Be sure to have a specific goal in mind for each training session you facilitate. What do you hope to accomplish? Take the time to put your goal into words, as it will then be more powerful and succinct. Do you plan to clearly state this goal at the beginning of the training session? Is your goal realistic? Have you realistically considered how much time you will need to reach this goal? How will you know if you have succeeded in meeting your goal? What evidence will you be looking for? All of these questions can assist you with staying focused and targeted as you work toward improving teaching and learning.

Making the Move from Current State Standards to Common Core Standards

When transitioning from current state standards to Common Core State Standards, there are many aspects that need careful consideration. It is important to invest some time comparing standards and planning how the transition from state standards to Common Core State Standards will occur.

Considerations
- What are the commonalities between current state standards and the Common Core State Standards? What are the differences?

- Where do gaps exist between the two?

- How will these gaps be addressed so that students can be successful when transitioning from state standards to Common Core State Standards?

- Are there concepts/areas of focus in current state standards that have been shifted to a different grade level or omitted completely within the Common Core State Standards? Has rigor increased?

- Has a time frame for transitioning from state standards to Common Core State Standards been determined? Has this plan been shared with all stakeholders?

- Is there a plan in place for a parent information session and/or newsletter in which the Common Core State Standards will be shared and explained?

Gap Analysis – Current State Standards and Common Core State Standards

Select one of the Gap Analysis Templates provided. Use this template to explore the similarities and differences between existing state standards and the Common Core State Standards.

Through this process, identify:

- Concepts or areas of focus found within state standards that are no longer required within the Common Core State Standards

- Concepts or areas of focus that have not previously been required within state standards at a particular grade level, but are now included in the Common Core State Standards

- An increase or decrease in academic rigor

- Prerequisite knowledge and skills students will need to master within each grade level to succeed in future grades.

- Areas of concern

- Topics that may require more or less instructional time

- Content area knowledge that may need to be developed and/or fine-tuned with staff.

Gap Analysis Instructions

<u>Materials needed</u>
A copy of current state standards
A copy of the Common Core State Standards
1 highlighter
Sticky notes
Gap Analysis Templates, 1-4

1. Choose the Gap Analysis Template you would like to work with.

2. Review your current state standards, and choose one area of focus.

3. Using your highlighter, identify any changes in content that will be made when moving from state standards to Common Core State Standards.

4. Use sticky notes to add thoughts and ideas as you identify similarities and differences found.

5. Look through the Common Core State Standards and state standards from previous grade levels. Note any prerequisite skills that will need to be infused within a grade level during transition year. There may be additional skills or concepts within the Common Core State Standards that were not included in previous state standards. These concepts will need to be addressed as students move from one set of standards to the other.

Gap Analysis Template 1

Subject_____
Grade Level_____
Area of focus _____

Current State Standard

[   ]

Common Core State Standard

[   ]

Current state standard component(s) no longer required within the Common Core State Standards

[   ]

New grade level component/area of focus required within the Common Core State Standards

[   ]

Gap Analysis Template 2

Subject_____
Grade Level _____
Area of focus_____

Common Core State Standard concept/area of focus
new to the grade level

Resources/ideas for incorporating this concept/area of focus

Gap Analysis Template 3

Subject _____
Grade Level _____
Area of focus_____

Gap found between state standard and Common Core State Standard

Strategies for addressing the gap found

Gap Analysis Template 4

Subject _____
Grade Level _____
Area of focus_____

New concept/area of focus included within Common Core State Standards

Prerequisite skills needed for this concept/area of focus

Strategies for addressing prerequisite skills during the transition year.

Comparison Template

Record a current state standard and a similar Common Core State Standard. Analyze the similarities and differences between the two.

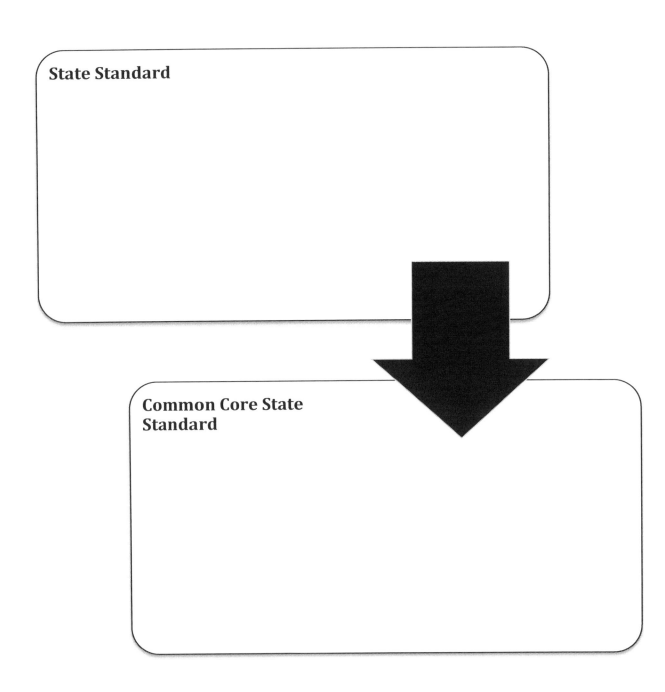

Chapter 5

Identifying Gaps Within the Curriculum

Comparing Curriculum Maps/Pacing Guides to the Common Core State Standards

This chapter contains a collection of strategies and templates to assist with comparing and contrasting academic requirements found in current curriculum maps and Common Core State Standards.

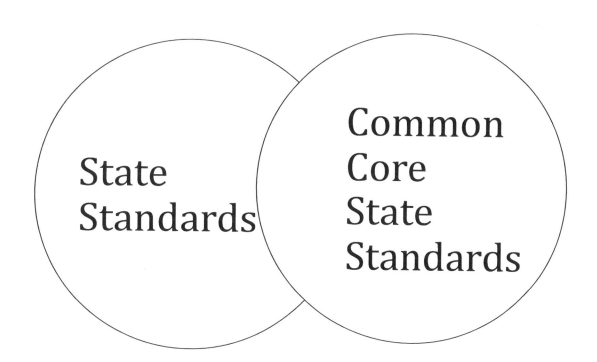

Gap Analysis (Curriculum/Pacing Guides)

Considerations

- What gaps are evident within the current curriculum map when the Common Core State Standards are considered?

- Does academic rigor increase/decrease/remain the same?

- How will these gaps be addressed so that students can be successful when transitioning from one grade level to the next, considering the expectations found within the Common Core State Standards?

- Are there concepts/areas of focus in current grade level curriculum maps that have been shifted to a different grade level or omitted completely within the Common Core State Standards?

- Has a time frame for transitioning from the current curriculum map to a new map based on the Common Core State Standards been determined? Has this plan been shared with all stakeholders?

- Is there a plan in place for a parent information session and/or newsletter in which the Common Core State Standards will be shared and explained? Can this information be posted on the school or district website?

Steps for Analyzing Current Curriculum Maps in regard to the Common Core State Standards

Select one of the Gap Analysis templates provided. Use the template to explore the similarities and differences between existing curriculum maps and the Common Core State Standards.

Through this process, identify:

- Concepts or areas of focus found within the curriculum map that are no longer required within Common Core State Standards

- Concepts or areas of focus that have not previously been required within the curriculum map at a particular grade level, but are now included in the Common Core State Standards

- The level of academic rigor required

- Prerequisite knowledge and skills students will need to master within each grade level to succeed in future grades.

- Areas of concern

- Topics that may require more or less instructional time

- Areas that may require additional instructional resources

Gap Analysis Instructions

<u>Materials needed</u>
A copy of the current curriculum map
A copy of the Common Core State Standards
Gap Analysis Template (Choose one)

1. Choose the Gap Analysis Template you would like to work with.

2. Review your current curriculum map, beginning with September.

3. Choose a Common Core State Standard to focus on. Walk through the curriculum map and identify lessons, units, and supplemental materials that address this particular Common Core State Standard. Record the lessons/units that match.

4. Record if the match is weak or strong

5. Determine the academic rigor of the Common Core State Standard. Is it the same, lower or higher than the current state standards?

6. Note any prerequisite skills that will need to be infused within a grade level during the transition year. There may be additional skills or concepts within the Common Core State Standards that were not included in previous state standards/curriculum maps. These concepts will need to be addressed as the transition is made from one set of standards to the other.

Gap Analysis Template 5

Subject_____

Grade Level_____

Common Core State Standard

Location in Current Curriculum Map	Rigor	Notes

Gap Analysis Template 6

Subject_____
Grade Level _____

Common Core State Standards Not Found in Current Curriculum Map

1.

2.

3.

4.

5.

6.

7.

Gap Analysis Template 7

Subject_____

Grade Level _____

Identify a Common Core State Standard not found in the current curriculum map.

[ ]

List resources/ideas for incorporating this concept/area of focus into the revised curriculum map.

[ ]

Gap Analysis Template 8

Subject_____
Grade Level _____

Identify a concept/area of focus that will be added to the new curriculum map.

List prerequisite skills needed for this concept/area of focus.

List strategies for addressing these prerequisite skills during the transition year.

Chapter 6

Analyzing Current Student Work Samples to Find Evidence of Common Core State Standards Rigor.

An effective method of assessing the capabilities of current students as well as current expectations is to look at a snapshot of their work. Consider these questions as you begin your analysis:
- What can the artifact tell us about student understanding?
- Does the task address content outlined in the Common Core State Standards?
- Does the rigor need to be increased?
- What specific content needs to be expanded upon, omitted, or moved to another grade level?

Analyzing authentic student work is an effective method of determining current expectations. Artifacts include any student work sample that can provide the teacher with information about student understanding, learning, and/or application. Artifacts include items such as essays, open-ended problems, extended constructed response problems, projects, presentations, diagrams, charts, recordings, and experiments.

Working Through the Process

To begin the process of analyzing student artifacts, collect a sampling of current student work. Samples should include students from different classrooms when possible, who are at varying levels. Next, begin to analyze the artifacts through the lens of Common Core State Standards. This snapshot can provide teachers and administrators with critical information as to how the rigor of the task compares to the rigor found in Common Core State Standards.

Time spent reflecting upon the results of this type of analysis plays a critical role in understanding the depth of the CCSS.
The key to successfully analyzing work samples is to identify the objective of the assignment, and compare it with a similar standard found in the Common Core. Determine if it is being met, the rigor of the current objective, the instructional approach used to initially teach the concept, and the effectiveness of the lesson.

Choose one of the templates provided to record the results of the analysis. Use precise, clear language when writing notes, and highlight where the evidence of rigor can be found. Additional comments can be written on a sticky note, in a notebook, or on a class recording sheet. Some teachers find it is easier to make a photocopy of the artifact so that they can write directly on the work sample. Different color inks can be used to indicate where there may be an increase or decrease in expectations. A highlighter can be used to identify content no longer required at a grade level, or content that is new to a grade level.

Analysis of Student Work Sample (Template #1)

What is the teaching point for this artifact?	Does the rigor align with the CCSS? If so, how?
	If not, what areas are different?

Rewrite the task so that it meets the rigor of the Common Core Standards

Student Work Sample Analysis (Template #2)

Describe the Artifact	Record the Task

Common Core Standard (s) being addressed

Observations & Insights

1.

2.

3.

Ways to Increase the Rigor

1.

2.

3.

Next Steps

Student Work Sample Analysis (Template #3)

Was the content and format of the task appropriate in terms of the spirit of the Common Core State Standard? Explain.
What content needs to be added/deleted so that the rigor is appropriate for the grade level?
What prerequisite skills are needed for students to successfully complete this task?
Which instructional strategies would be effective for teaching the lesson in the future?
Are there additional materials that could be used to effectively teach the objective?

Identifying Strategies for Increasing Rigor

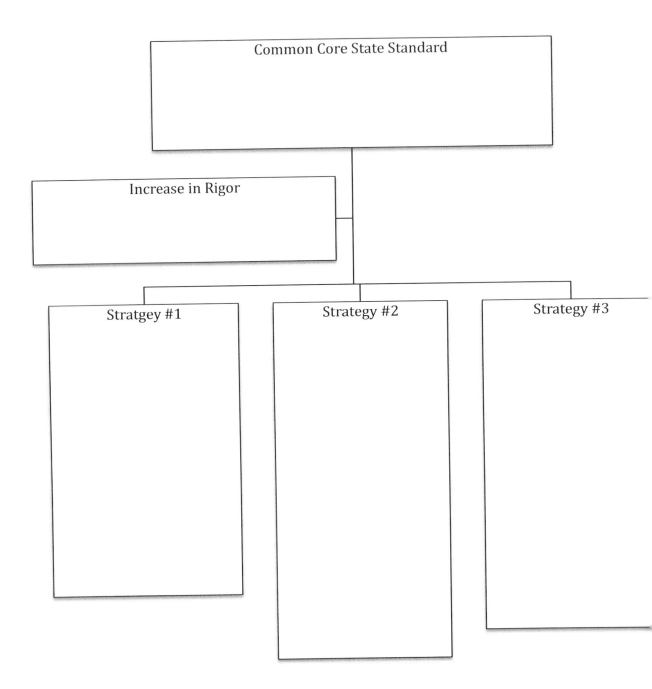

Notes

Notes

Made in the USA
Lexington, KY
17 April 2011